easy going
locker zu super Noten

Schulaufgaben

von bayerischen Gymnasien

Englisch 5

nach neuem Lehrplan PLUS und G9

mit Lösungen

DURCHBLICKER Lernstudio Arndt

Schulaufgaben von bayerischen Gymnasien

Verfügbare Titel

☺ **Mathematik** für Klasse **5, 6, 7, 8, 9, 10, 11** und **12**

☺ **Physik** für Klasse **8, 9** und **10**

☺ **Chemie** für Klasse **8, 9** und **10**

☺ **Englisch** für Klasse **5, 6, 7, 8, 9, 10** und **11/12**

☺ **Französisch** für Klasse **6, 7, 8** und **9**

☺ **Deutsch** für Klasse **5, 6, 7** und **8**

☺ **Latein** für Lernjahr **1, 2** und **3**

Schulaufgaben bayerischer Realschulen

Verfügbare Titel

☺ **Mathematik** für Klasse **5, 6, $7_{II/III}$, $8_{II/III}$, $9_{II/III}$** und **$10_{II/III}$**

☺ **Englisch** für Klasse **5, 6, 7, 8, 9** und **10**

☺ **Deutsch** für Klasse **5, 6, 7** und **8**

Schulproben von bayerischen Grundschulen

Verfügbare Titel

☺ **Mathematik** für Klasse **3** und **4**

☺ **Deutsch** für Klasse **3** und **4**

☺ **Heimat- und Sachunterricht (HSU)** für Klasse **3** und **4**

Vorwort

Liebe Schüler, liebe Eltern,

seit das G9 wieder eingeführt worden ist, gibt es ganz neue Englischbücher. Die hier vorliegenden Aufgaben entsprechen voll und ganz dem neu eingeführten **Lehrplan*PLUS***, Grundlage von **G9**. Die englische Sprache ist dadurch praxisnäher und lebendiger geworden. Diese

Schulaufgaben von bayerischen Gymnasien
Englisch 5

zeigen, welcher Schwierigkeitsgrad heute im Gymnasium in Bayern verlangt wird. Ein großer Teil der Aufgabentypen habe ich als Englischlehrerin selbst entworfen. Original-Schulaufgaben von Nachhilfeschülern unseres ***Durchblicker Lernstudio Arndt*** bilden die Grundlage der Aufgaben in diesem Buch. Wer diese Schulaufgaben konsequent durcharbeitet, dem sind bessere Noten sicher. Zumindest weiß man, wie die Aufgaben aussehen können. Durch Übung kommt jeder Schüler zum Erfolg.

In der 5. Klasse werden vier Schulaufgaben geschrieben. Oft heißen diese dann „Großer Leistungstest". Im vorliegenden Band finden sich pro Schulaufgabe jeweils zwei Prüfungen. Die acht hier gestellten Schulaufgaben mit Lösungen entsprechen dem hohen Niveau aus Gymnasien in Bayern, die das

Schülerbuch Green Line 1

im Unterricht verwenden und sie basieren auf tatsächlich gestellten Aufgaben.

Als Schüler kennst du ***Vocabulary*** mit Übungen zu Vokabeln und ***Grammar*** mit Übungen zur Grammatik. ***Speaking*** lernst du zum Training der Sprachfertigkeit. ***Writing*** übst du durch ***Text Production*** sowie ***Dictation*** und schulst das Schreiben mit Diktatübungen. ***Dialogue, Mediation*** und ***Composition*** dient zur Übersetzung ins Englische. ***Listening*** verbessert das Hörverstehen.

Mit diesem Band kannst du Schritt für Schritt alle Schulaufgaben durcharbeiten, bis du fit bist für die nächste Schulaufgabe. Wenn sich die Fehler häufen, dann musst du verstärkt Vokabeln lernen oder in der Grammatik oder im Schülerbuch noch einmal die Kapitel, um die es geht, wiederholen. Mein Ziel ist es, die Motivation und Kreativität aller Schüler beim Lösen von Schulaufgaben in Englisch zu fördern. Dazu biete ich die **ausführliche Lösung** der Aufgabenstellung.

Viel Spaß beim Lösen der Schulaufgaben

Deine und Ihre Englischtrainerin Monika Arndt

Aussage einer Mutter am 13.09.2013: **„Mein Sohn Leander hat sich schon letztes Jahr ausschließlich mit Ihren Heften auf seine Schulaufgaben in Mathe und Englisch vorbereitet, was uns zu einem insgesamt recht entspannten ersten Schuljahr im Gymnasium verholfen hat. Wir erleben Ihre Hefte als echte Unterstützung!"**

Monika Arndt (Dipl.-Übersetzerin) veröffentlichte als Buchautorin Ernährungsbücher für Kinder in den Verlagen dtv und Ravensburger. **Das Baby-Kochbuch**, **Wie Kinder fit und gesund bleiben** und **Das Ravensburger Kochbuch für Kinder** mit Bildern von Ali Mitgutsch.
Zuvor hat Monika Arndt in verschiedenen Redaktionen gearbeitet, z.B. über zehn Jahre in der Redaktion des Schulfernsehheftes beim Bayerischen Schulfernsehen. Beim Stark-Verlag hat sie über Produktion und Inhalt von Lernhilfen Erfahrungen gesammelt, geeignete Lehrer gesucht und die Bücher als Lektorin redigiert.
Sie unterrichtet Englisch und Französisch im ***Durchblicker Lernstudio Arndt***.

Titelbild: Heinrich Schmid, Überlingen am Ried / Singen am Hohentwiel
www.durchblicker.org

ISBN **978-3-00-034520-3**

9 783000 345203

1. Schulaufgabe aus dem Englischen

Name: ______________________________

Stoff: Unit 1, Unit 2

I. Dictation *(Zahlen aus Lösung 2x vorlesen lassen)*

Listen to the information and write down the correct number(s)

1. What is Linda's phone number? ______________________
2. How old is Tom? ______________________
3. What is Marcos favourite number? ______________________
4. How many dogs has Anna? ______________________

____/8

II. Vocabulary

1. Fill in the missing vocabulary words

a) Green, red and pink are ________________.

b) My mum and dad are my ________________.

c) What is your favourite ________________? – It's dogs.

d) I don't have a sister or brother – I am an ________________.

e) My sister speaks two ________________: English and German.

f) We live in a house with a ________________.

g) Do you ________________ our new teacher's name?

h) Bears are ________, worms are small.

____/8

2. Translate these sentences into English

a) Es sind überall Meerschweinchen.

____

b) Wir haben keinen Herd in der Küche.

____

c) Meine kleine Schwester ist immer nett.

My little sister is always nice

d) Vier und neunzehn ist dreiundzwanzig.

four and nineteen is twenty-three

____/8

III. Grammar

1. Write the plural form of the following words

a) mouse – mice
b) girl – girls
c) family – families
d) worm – worms
e) sentence – sentences
f) number – numbers

____/6

2. Fill in the missing personal pronouns and forms of be (positive and negative)

a) Marc is my brother, but isn't my friend.
b) No, Linda and I ________________ fourteen. __________ twelve years old.
c) They ________ from Munich and ______________ really nice.
d) ______ you new at this school? Yes, ______________________.
e) I ________________ happy, _______ very angry.

____/10

IV. Text Production

Write a short text about yourself. You can be creative. You can use the ideas in the box but you can come up with your own ideas
Schreibe einen kurzen Text über dich selbst. Du kannst die Ideen aus der Box benutzen, dir aber auch eigene Ideen ausdenken

Name – family – hobbies – favourite animal / colour / number / sport… – Where do you live? – school – activities…

Hello, my name is Johannes. My family is great. My favourite kuddly toy is Bärli. My hobbys are swimming and football. My favourite colour is blue. My favourite numbers are fifteen, one, seven, ten and three. I have a little brother one father and one mother and one parents.
I am, You are, He is, She is, It is, Were are You are, Tey are
We are

____/20

Total ____/60

Good luck !

Lösung: 1. Schulaufgabe aus dem Englischen

I. Dictation *(Zahlen 2x vorlesen lassen)*

Listen to the information and write down the correct number(s).

1. What is Linda's phone number? *1 8 7 5 5 6 9*
2. How old is Tom? *13*
3. What is Marcos favourite number? *12*
4. How many dogs has Anna? *3*

Tipps und Hinweise
Falls du dir bei einer der Zahlen während des Zuhörens nicht ganz sicher bist und sie nicht direkt richtig aufschreiben kannst, schreibe dir einfach eine kurze Notiz mit Bleistift (z.B. das was du hörst, also die Aussprache der Zahl). Versuche dich dann einfach nach einiger Zeit nochmal zu erinnern, welche Zahl es ist oder zähle leise im Kopf vor dich hin.

II. Vocabulary

1. Fill in the missing vocabulary words

a) Green, red and pink are *colours.*

b) My mum and dad are my *parents.*

c) What is your favourite *animal?* – It's dogs.

d) I don't have a sister or brother – I am an *only child.*

e) My sister speaks two *languages:* English and German.

f) We live in a house with a *garden.*

g) Do you *remember* our new teacher's name?

h) Bears are *big*, worms are small.

2. Translate these sentences into English

a) Es sind überall Meerschweinchen. *There are guinea pigs everywhere.*

b) Wir haben keinen Herd in der Küche. *We don't have a cooker in the kitchen.*

c) Meine kleine Schwester ist immer nett. *My little sister is always nice.*

d) Vier und neunzehn ist dreiundzwanzig. *Four plus nineteen is twenty-three.*

Tipps und Hinweise
Die **Personalpronomen** können für Menschen, Gegenstände, Tiere und Begriffe stehen.
Es gibt folgende Personalpronomen:
I, you, he, she, it, we, you, they
Die **Possessivpronomen** zeigen dir, wem etwas gehört. Sie stehen vor einem Nomen.
Es gibt folgende Possessivpronomen:
I – my, you – your, he – his, she – her, it – its, we – our, you – your, they – their

III. Grammar

1. Write the plural form of the following words

a) mouse – *mice*

b) girl – *girls*

c) family – *families*

d) worm – *worms*

e) sentence – *sentences*

f) number – *numbers*

Das muss ich wissen
Im Englischen benutzt du den **Plural** (wie im Deutschen), wenn du von mehreren Personen oder Sachen sprichst. Der Plural wird in der Regel bei fast allen Nomen durch ein einfaches Anhängen des Buchstaben ***-s*** gebildet:
z.B. *one boy – two boys* *a cat – three cats*
Aber Achtung! Einige Wörter haben eine besondere Schreibweise und bilden Ausnahmen. Diese solltest du dir auswendig merken.
Einige Beispiele sind: *mouse – mice; family – families; hobby – hobbies*

2. Fill in the missing personal pronouns and forms of be (positive and negative)

a) Marc *isn't* my brother, but *he is* my friend.

b) No, Linda and I *aren't* fourteen. *We are* twelve years old.

c) They *are* from Munich and *they're* really nice.

d) *Are* you new at this school? Yes, *I am / we are.*

e) I *am not* happy, *I'm* very angry.

Tipps und Hinweise
Bei dieser Aufgabe ist es egal, ob du die **Kurzform** oder **Langform** schreibst. Falls du also in Satz c) *they are really nice* schreibst, gibt das trotzdem die volle Punktzahl!
Bei Satz d) ist nicht eindeutig, ob sich die Frage an eine oder mehrere Personen richtet, hier darfst du also frei entscheiden, ob du im zweiten Teil *Yes, I am* oder *Yes, we are* schreibst.

Das muss ich wissen

Im Englischen gibt es folgende Personalpronomen:

Singular:	ich – *I*	du – *you*	er – *he*	sie – *she*	es – *it*
Plural:	wir – *we*	ihr – *you*		sie – *they*	

Mit den Personalpronomen und der passenden Form von *(to) be* kannst du sagen, wer oder was jemand /etwas ist. Es gibt jeweils eine Langform und eine Kurzform.

Langform	**Kurzform**
I am	*I'm*
you are	*you're*
he is	*he's*
she is	*she's*
it is	*it's*
we are	*we're*
you are	*you're*
they are	*they're*

Verwendest du die Personalpronomen, die dazugehörige Form von *(to) be* und *not* kannst du sagen, was jemand / etwas nicht ist. Auch hier gibt es wieder jeweils eine Langform und eine Kurzform.

Langform	**Kurzform**
I am not	*I'm not*
you are not	*you aren't*
he is not	*he isn't*
she is not	*she isn't*
it is not	*it isn't*
we are not	*we aren't*
you are not	*you aren't*
they are not	*they aren't*

IV. Text Production

Write a short text about yourself. You can be creative. You can use the ideas in the box but you can come up with your own ideas

Schreibe einen kurzen Text über dich selbst. Du kannst die Ideen aus der Box benutzen, dir aber auch eigene Ideen ausdenken

Name – family – hobbies – favourite animal / colour / number / sport… - where do you live? – school – activities …

My name is Linda. I live in Berlin with my family. I have two sisters and one brother. I am twelve years old. I love concerts. My favourite animals are squirrels and snakes. My favourite colour is green. I have a dog. Her name is Stacy.

1. Schulaufgabe aus dem Englischen

Name: ____________________________

Stoff: Unit 1, Unit 2, Unit 3 (nur Vokabeln)

I. Listening Comprehension

Listen to the text and answer all questions by completing the sentences
Höre dem Text zu und beantworte alle Fragen, indem du Sätze vervollständigst
(Text in Lösung 2x vorlesen lassen)

1. The short name for the school is TTS.
2. The school has a new cafeteria and a big computer room
3. The board is new in the classroom.
4. All students have to read the class rules at home.
5. The students at Thomas Tallis School wear blue uniforms.
6. There is a school shop where you can buy pens, notebooks or sweets.
7. For the English class all students need a new English book and an orange exercise book
8. There is a welcome party in the cafeteria right now.

____/12

II. Vocabulary

Find the opposites to these words. ***Finde die Gegensätze dieser Wörter***

uncle ↔ aunt
rude ↔ polite
small ↔ big
to go to bed ↔ to get up
never ↔ always
morning ↔ evening
last ↔ first
hello ↔ ~~So Bey~~ Bye
late ↔ early
man ↔ wommen

____/10

III. Grammar

1. Fill in the correct form of *a / an*

Marla this is a picture of my family. – Oh, it is an absolutely great picture.

You can see a girl with a man.

We have an English test on Monday and you all have to bring a uniform.

____/6

2. Fill in the correct personal pronouns and possessive determiners

a) Look, this is my cat. Her name is Lizzy.

b) What colour is your pencil case? – ~~Its~~ It is green and blue.

c) My friend Max is great. His room is very big.

d) My parents are from India.

e) This is Mr Swindon. He is my new tutor for this year.

f) Look at the snake, ~~His~~ Its eyes are yellow.

g) ~~Her~~ Your mom is very nice, Toni. I like ~~his~~ her smile.

____/10

IV. Translation

1. In English, please! Was sagst du, wenn du...

a) jemanden fragen willst, wie er/sie heißt?

____

b) jemanden fragen willst, wie alt er/sie ist?

____

c) jemanden fragen willst, wann er/sie Geburtstag hat?

____

d) fragen willst, wer auf dem Foto ist?

____

e) fragen willst, wo die Thomas Tallis Schule ist?

____

f) fragen willst, wer deine Lehrerin ist?

____

____/12

V. Text Production

Write a short text (five sentences) about your school and / or class

____

____

____

____

____

____

____/10

Total ____/60

Good luck !

to swim
to play
to eat
to cook

to

too

Lösung: 1. Schulaufgabe aus dem Englischen

I. Listening Comprehension

Listen to the text and answer all questions by completing the sentences
Höre dem Text zu und beantworte alle Fragen, indem du Sätze vervollständigst
(Text 2x vorlesen lassen)

It is the first day at Thomas Tallis School. Mr Swindon is the tutor for this year. He tells the class some things about the school.

Mr Swindon: Good morning, students. Welcome to Thomas Tallis School, short TTS. I am happy about our new cafeteria and the big computer room. In our classroom we have a new white board. Please read the class rules at home. All students wear their blue uniform in school. In our school shop you can buy pens, notebooks and other things like sweets. For our English class you all need the new English book and the orange exercise book. Now let's go to the cafeteria for the welcome party.

1. The short name for the school is *TTS.*
2. The school has a new *computer room* and *a cafeteria.*
3. The *white board* is new in the classroom.
4. All students have to read the *classroom rules* at home.
5. The students at Thomas Tallis School wear *blue* uniforms.
6. There is a school shop where you can buy *pens*, *notebooks* or *sweets.*
7. For the English class all students need *the new English book* and *the orange exercise book.*
8. There is a *welcome party* in the cafeteria right now.

II. Vocabulary

Find the opposites to these words. Finde die Gegensätze dieser Wörter

uncle ↔ *aunt*
rude ↔ *polite*
small ↔ *big*
to go to bed ↔ *to get up*
never ↔ *always*
morning ↔ *evening*
last ↔ *first*
hello ↔ *goodbye*
late ↔ *early*
man ↔ *woman*

Tipps und Hinweise
Es ist oftmals hilfreich sich Vokabeln in Zusammenhängen zu merken. Gegensätze eignen sich hierfür z.B. besonders gut.

III. Grammar

1. Fill in the correct form of a / an

1. Marla this is *a* picture of my family. – Oh, it is *an* absolutely great picture.
2. You can see *a* girl with *a* man.
3. We have *an* English test on Monday and you all have to bring *a* uniform.

Das muss ich wissen
Der unbestimmte Artikel ***a*** wird von Konsonanten und ***an*** vor Vokalen genutzt. Achtung! Dabei zählt die Aussprache und nicht die Schreibweise (z.B. *a uniform, an uncle*).

2. Fill in the correct personal pronouns and possessive determiners

a) Look, this is *my* cat. *Her* name is Lizzy.

b) What colour is your pencil case? – *It* is green and blue.

c) My friend Max is great. *His* room is very big.

d) *My* parents are from India.

e) This is Mr Swindon. *He* is *our* new tutor for this year.

f) Look at the snake, *its* eyes are yellow.

g) *Your* mom is very nice, Toni. I like *her* smile.

Das musst du wissen
Die einfache Form der **Gegenwart** heißt ***simple present***.
Bei *I, you, we* und *they* haben Verben im ***simple present*** keine Endung.
Aber <u>Achtung</u>: Bei *he, she* und *it* wird an die Verben ein ***s*** angefügt *(he likes)*
Als Merksatz kannst du dir merken: *he, she, it* – das *s* muss mit!
Es gibt aber auch einige Ausnahmen. Diese musst du alle auswendig kennen!
Beim Hilfsverb *can* wird bei *he / she / it* kein ***s*** angehängt! *(She can talk to us.)*
Bei Verben die auf den **Konsonanten *-y*** enden wird, das ***y + s*** im ***simple present*** zu ***-ies***
(to try → she tries)
Das Verb *to have* wird im ***simple present*** bei *he / she / it* zu *has → she has*
An das Verb *to go* wird ein ***-es*** angehängt *(she goes)*
An das Verb *to do* wird ein ***-es*** angehängt *(she does)*
Um Aussagen im ***simple present*** zu verneinen, nutzt du *don't* + **Infinitiv** bzw. *doesn't* + **Infinitiv**
I don't like *you don't like* *he doesn't like* *she doesn't like*
we don't like *you don't like* *they don't like*
<u>Achtung</u>: Hier wird dann bei der 3. Person Singular *(he / she / it)* kein ***s*** ans Verb gehängt.

IV. Translation

1. In English, please! Was sagst du, wenn du...

a) jemanden fragen willst, wie er/sie heißt?

What is your name? / What's your name?

b) jemanden fragen willst, wie alt er/sie ist?

How old are you?

c) jemanden fragen willst, wann er/sie Geburtstag hat?

When is your birthday?

d) fragen willst, wer auf dem Foto ist?

Who is in the picture / photograph?

e) fragen willst, wo die Thomas Tallis Schule ist?

Where is Thomas Tallis School?

f) fragen willst, wer deine Lehrerin ist?

Who is my teacher?

Das muss ich wissen
Wenn du bestimmte Informationen erhalten möchtest, brauchst du Fragewörter, mit denen du danach fragen kannst:
Wo…? – Where…?
Woher… ? – Where … from?
Wer…? – Who…?
Was…? – What…?
Wie alt…? – How old…?

Oft kannst du nach einem Fragewort die verkürzte Form von Fragewort + *(to) be* nutzen
z.B. *Where is → Where's*
Who is… → Who's

V. Text Production

Write a short text (five sentences) about your school and / or class

I go to Michaeli-Gymnasium in Munich. I am in grade 5. There are twelve girls and seventeen boys in my class. My teacher's name is Ms Regelhaupt. My favourite subjects are English, Math and Biology.

2. Schulaufgabe aus dem Englischen

Name: ____________________________

Stoff: Unit 3, Unit 4

I. Reading Comprehension

Read the following text. Answer all questions. Tick the correct boxes

There are many kids in our street. When they come home from school they all do their homework. Lincy has a dog. She often goes for a walk with her dog in the park. Roberto has a dog, too. He never goes for a walk with his dog. Andy and Aless play together with their sisters. Onur likes to watch TV. Marga has to help her mom in the kitchen. After that she likes to watch TV. Mirko plays with his big brother. Roberto sometimes cooks. Lincy, Andy and Onur have dinner with their families. Aless listens to Music. Marga's parents come home in the evening. Andy's mom works at home. Mirko's cousin has a dog. He sometimes goes for a walk with his cousin's dog.

Who...	**Lincy**	**Roberto**	**Andy**	**Aless**	**Onur**	**Mirko**	**Marga**
… goes for a walk with his/her dog?							
… does his/her homework?							
… listens to music?							
… plays with his/her sister/brother?							
… watches TV?							
… eats dinner with the family?							
… helps his/her mom ?							
… cooks?							

____/20

II. Vocabulary

1. What's the time? Write what time it is in a full sentence

Wie viel Uhr ist es? Schreibe in einem ganzen Satz, wie viel Uhr es ist

a) 8:00 → ____________________

b) 4:25 → ____________________

c) 5:57 → ____________________

d) 10:45 → ____________________

e) 7:30 → ____________________

f) 2:17 → ____________________ ____/6

2. Write the plural form of these words. ***Schreibe den Plural dieser Wörter***

a) man – men

b) country – countries

c) story – stories

d) foot – feet

e) woman – women

f) sheep – sheep

____/6

III. Grammar

1. Fill in: ***it's – its – you're – your – they're – their – there***

______ Friday afternoon and the Millers are in ________ living room. _________ are Mr Miller, Mrs Miller, Fanny and _________ dog. ______ name is Fluffy. Mr and Mrs Miller smile. ____________ happy and Mr Miller says: "Fanny, ____________ a great daughter. Thanks for ________ help this afternoon."

____/8

2. Complete this text. Use the simple past of these words
Vervollständige diesen Text und benutze die einfache Form der Vergangenheit dieser Wörter

buy – get angry – go – laugh – tell – make fun of – say – show

Last weekend, Clarissa ____________ to the shopping mall. She _____________ a new dress and new shoes. Clarissa ______________ her brothers her new dress. They ___________________ her and her little brother ___________ a lot. Clarissa ________________________ at him and _____________ their mum about it. Her mum ___________: "Clarissa, don't worry, darling. I love your new dress."

____/8

IV. Text Production

Write a short text about a regular day in your life. What do you usually / always / sometimes / often / never do. Write at least five sentences

Schreibe einen Text über einen normalen Tag in deinem Leben. Schreibe darüber, was du gewöhnlich, manchmal, selten, oft, nie tust. Schreibe mindestens fünf Sätze

____

____

____

____

____

____

____

____

____

_____/20

Total ____/68

Good luck !

Lösung: 2. Schulaufgabe aus dem Englischen

I. Reading Comprehension

Read the following text. Answer all questions. Tick the correct boxes

There are many kids in our street. When they come home from school they all do their homework. Lincy has a dog. She often goes for a walk with her dog in the park. Roberto has a dog, too. He never goes for a walk with his dog. Andy and Aless play together with their sisters. Onur likes to watch TV. Marga has to help her mom in the kitchen. After that she likes to watch TV. Mirko plays with his big brother. Roberto sometimes cooks. He likes to listen to music when he cooks. Lincy, Andy and Onur have dinner with their families. Aless listens to Music. Marga cooks dinner for her sister and brother. Andy's mom works at home. Mirko's cousin has a dog. He sometimes goes for a walk with his cousin's dog.

Who...	**Lincy**	**Roberto**	**Andy**	**Aless**	**Onur**	**Mirko**	**Marga**
… goes for a walk with his/her dog?	*x*						
… does his/her homework?	*x*	*x*	*x*	*x*	*x*	*x*	*x*
… listens to music?		*x*		*x*			
… plays with his/her sister/brother?			*x*	*x*		*x*	
… watches TV?					*x*		*x*
… eats dinner with the family?	*x*		*x*		*x*		
… helps his/her mom ?							*x*
… cooks?		*x*					*x*

Tipps und Hinweise

Achtung, hier sind ein paar Fallen eingebaut, um zu sehen, ob du den Text genau gelesen hast. Beispielsweise geht Mirko mit einem Hund spazieren – aber nicht mit seinem.

→ Die Frage lautet aber wer mit <u>seinem</u> Hund spazieren geht. Du musst den Text also ganz genau lesen und überprüfen, ob du die richtigen Angaben angekreuzt hast.

II. Vocabulary

1. What's the time? Write what time it is in a full sentence

Wie viel Uhr ist es? Schreibe in einem ganzen Satz wie viel Uhr es ist

a) 8:00 → *It's eight o'clock.*

b) 4:25 → *It's twenty-five past four.*

c) 5:57 → *It's three minutes to six. / It's five fifty-seven.*

d) 10:45 → *It's quarter to eleven.*

e) 7:30 → *It's half past seven.*

f) 2:17 → *It's seventeen minutes past two.*

2. Write the plural form of these words. *Schreibe den Plural dieser Wörter*

a) man – *men*

b) country – *countries*

c) story – *stories*

d) foot – *feet*

e) woman – *women*

f) sheep – *sheep*

III. Grammar

1. Fill in: *it's – its – you're – your – they're – their – there*

It's Friday afternoon and the Millers are in *their* living room. *There* are Mr Miller, Mrs Miller, Fanny and *their* dog. *Its* name is Fluffy. Mr and Mrs Miller smile. *They're* happy and Mr Miller says: "Fanny, *you're* a great daughter. Thanks for *your* help this afternoon."

2. Complete this text. Use the simple past of these words
Vervollständige diesen Text und benutze die einfache Form der Vergangenheit dieser Wörter

buy – get angry – go – laugh – tell – make fun of – say – show

Last weekend, Clarissa *went* to the shopping mall. She *bought* a new dress and new shoes. Clarissa *showed* her brothers her new dress. They *made fun of* her and her little brother *laughed* a lot. Clarissa *got angry* at him and *told* their mum about it. Her mum *said:* "Clarissa, don't worry, darling. I love your new dress."

Das muss ich wissen
Die einfache Form der **Vergangenheit** (das ***simple past***) wird in der Regel gebildet, indem du den Verben ein ***ed*** an den **Infinitiv** hängst.
z.B. *to play → played*
Diese Form wird dann für alle Personen verwendet.
Also: *I / you / he / she / it / we / you / they played in the snow.*
Es gibt aber auch Sonderformen:
Bei Verben mit stummem ***e*** am Ende z.B. *arrive* fällt dieses weg → *arrived*
Bei Verben mit einzelnem betontem Vokal wird der Konsonant verdoppelt z.B. *stop → stopped*
Bei Verben mit ***y*** nach Konsonant verändert sich dieses zu einem ***-ied*** → *to try → tried*
Unregelmäßige Verben: es gibt einige Verben, bei denen die Vergangenheitsform unregelmäßig ist. Diese musst du auswendig lernen (z.B. *to go → went* oder *to come → came)*

IV. Text Production

Write a short text about a regular day in your life. What do you usually / always / sometimes / often / never do. Write at least five sentences
Schreibe einen Text über einen normalen Tag in deinem Leben. Schreibe darüber, was du gewöhnlich, manchmal, selten, oft, nie tust. Schreibe mindestens fünf Sätze

X

I usually get up at seven o'clock in the morning. I always eat cereal for breakfast. I go to school and sometimes I go to see my friends after school. I never want to tidy up my room.
I often play with my brother in the afternoon. I sometimes go to bed very late at midnight.

Das muss ich wissen
Mit den **Häufigkeitsadverbien** ***(adverbs of frequency)*** kannst du sagen, wie oft etwas passiert.
Dazu gehören ***always, usually, often, sometimes*** und ***never***.
Im Englischen stehen die Häufigkeitsadverbien in der Regel vor dem Vollverb.
Aber Achtung beim Verb *to be*: hier stehen die Häufigkeitsadverbien hinter *am / are / is*.
Sie stehen niemals zwischen dem Verb und Objekt. Verwendest du ein Hilfsverb wie z.B *can* stehen sie nach diesem. Benutzt du *have got* musst du das Häufigkeitsadverb zwischen *have* und *got* schreiben.
In verneinten Sätzen muss ***sometimes*** immer vor dem Hilfsverb bzw. vor *be* stehen.

2. Schulaufgabe aus dem Englischen

Name: ____________________________

Stoff: Unit 3, Unit 4

I. Listening Comprehension

Listen to the text and answer all the questions. Answer in complete sentences

(Text in Lösung 2x vorlesen lassen)

waiter = Bedienung

a) Where are Monti and Devon?

____

____

b) What does the waiter ask them?

____

____

c) What does Devon want for lunch?

____

____

d) What does Monti want to drink?

____

____

e) Who would like to drink milk?

____

____

____/15

II. Vocabulary

1. Translate into English. ***Übersetze ins Englische***

a) Es gibt wichtige Informationen auf Seite 7.

____

b) Vergiss nicht dein Gesicht zu waschen.

____

c) Wir müssen nach einer neuen Trainerin suchen.

____

d) Abends lese ich oft ein Buch.

____

____/12

III. Grammar

1. Use the adverbs of frequency and say this information in English
Verwende das passende Häufigkeitsadverb und sage diese Information auf Englisch

a) Sage, dass du normalerweise mit dem Bus zur Schule gehst.

____

b) Sage, dass er nie Zeit hat.

____

c) Sage, dass sie dienstags manchmal Tennis spielt.

____

d) Sage, dass wir nie zu spät sind.

____

e) Sage, dass deine Mutter oft sonntags arbeiten muss.

____

____/10

2. Write the questions to the given answers or the (short) answers to the given questions
Schreibe die Fragen zu den gegebenen Antworten oder die (Kurz-) Antworten zu den gegebenen Fragen

a) Do you live in Austria? – Yes, ______________________.

b) ________________________________? – No, he doesn't like bananas.

c) Do they know your parents? – No, ____________________.

d) Do you eat cereal for breakfast? – Yes, __________________.

e) ____? No, they come by bus and not by bike.

____/10

IV. Text Production

Write an email to your friend Emily and tell her about a trip to the restaurant
(You can make up this trip it does not have to be real)
Schreibe eine E-Mail an deine Freundin Emily und erzähle ihr von einem Restaurantbesuch. Du kannst diesen erfinden, er muss nicht wirklich stattgefunden haben. Stell dir einfach vor, wie es war, was du gegessen hast, mit wem du dort warst etc. und berichte Emily davon

____/20

Total ____/67

Good luck !

Lösung: 2. Schulaufgabe aus dem Englischen

I. Listening Comprehension

Listen to the text and answer all the questions. Answer in complete sentences
(Text 2x vorlesen lassen)

waiter = Bedienung

Monti and Devon are at a restaurant in London. They want to have lunch.
Devon: Monti what would you like to eat?
Monti: I don't know. I'd like vegetables or the soup but the fruit salad sounds yummy, too. Or maybe a scone? What about you?
Devon: Hm, I think I would like a sandwich with cheese and later cake or biscuits for dessert.
The waiter comes and asks: "What would you like to drink and eat?"
Devon: I would like a sandwich with cheese and a scone with cream and jam. And I'd like to drink water, please. And I would like a salad. Wait, no salad, just a sandwich and a scone.
Waiter: And you, Miss?
Monti: I'd like a soup and the roast beef with potatoes. And I will take a fruit salad with ice cream for dessert.
Waiter: And what would you like to drink?
Monti: I'd like a cup of tea and some water, please.

a) Where are Monti and Devon?
Monti and Devon are at a restaurant in London.
b) What does the waiter ask them?
What would you like to eat and drink?
c) What does Devon want for lunch?
Devon wants a sandwich with cheese and a scone with cream and jam. He wants to drink water.
d) What does Monti want to drink?
Monti would like to drink tea and water.
e) Who would like to drink milk?
No one would like to drink milk.

II. Vocabulary

1. Translate into English. *Übersetze ins Englische*

a) Es gibt wichtige Informationen auf Seite 7.

There is important information on page seven.

b) Vergiss nicht dein Gesicht zu waschen.

Don't forget to wash your face.

c) Wir müssen nach einer neuen Trainerin suchen.

We have to look for a new trainer.

d) Abends lese ich oft ein Buch.

In the evenings, I often read a book.

Tipps und Hinweise
Achte darauf, dass es im Englischen für das Wort Information keine Mehrzahl gibt!

Tipps und Hinweise
Wenn du sagen möchtest, was du oder eine andere Person tun **muss**, verwendest du im Englischen das Verb ***(to) have to***.
Wichtig ist es, dass nach dem *have* immer das *to* stehen muss.
I have to
you have to
he / she / it has to Achtung: für die 3. Person Singular gibt es wieder eine besondere Form!
we have to
you have to
they have to
Fragen, verneinte Sätze und Kurzantworten werden mit *do / does* gebildet.
I don't have to
you don't have to
he / she / it doesn't have to
we don't have to
you don't have to
they don't have to

Do I have to...? – Yes, I do. / No, I don't.
Do you have to...? – Yes, you do. / No, you don't.
Does he / she / it have to...? – Yes, he / she / it does. / No, he / she / it doesn't.
Do we have to...? – Yes, we do. / No, we don't.
Do you have to...? – Yes, you do. / No, you don't.
Do they have to ...? – Yes, they do. / No, they don't.

III. Grammar

1. Use the adverbs of frequency and say this information in English
Verwende das passende Häufigkeitsadverb und sage diese Information auf Englisch

a) Sage, dass du normalerweise mit dem Bus zur Schule gehst.
I usually go to school by bus.
b) Sage, dass er nie Zeit hat.
He has never got time.
c) Sage, dass sie dienstags manchmal Tennis spielt.
She sometimes plays tennis on Tuesdays.
d) Sage, dass wir nie zu spät im Büro sind.
We are never late at the office.
e) Sage, dass deine Mutter oft sonntags arbeiten muss.
My mum often has to work on Sundays.

Das muss ich wissen
Mit den **Häufigkeitsadverbien** ***(adverbs of frequency)*** kannst du sagen, wie oft etwas passiert. Dazu gehören ***always, usually, often, sometimes*** und ***never***.
Im Englischen stehen die Häufigkeitsadverbien in der Regel vor dem Vollverb.
Aber Achtung beim Verb *to be*: Hier stehen die Häufigkeitsadverbien hinter *am / are / is*.
Sie stehen niemals zwischen dem Verb und Objekt. Verwendest du ein Hilfsverb wie z.B *can* stehen sie nach diesem. Benutzt du *have got* musst du das Häufigkeitsadverb zwischen *have* und *got* schreiben.
In verneinten Sätzen muss ***sometimes*** immer vor dem Hilfsverb bzw. vor *be* stehen.

2. Write the questions to the given answers or the (short) answers to the given questions
Schreibe die Fragen zu den gegebenen Antworten oder die (Kurz-) Antworten zu den gegebenen Fragen

a) Do you live in Austria? – Yes, *I do.*

b) *Does he like bananas*? – No, he doesn't like bananas.

c) Do they know your parents? – No, *they don't.*

d) Do you eat cereal for breakfast? – Yes, *I do.*

e) Do they come by bike? – No, they come by bus and not by bike.

Tipps und Hinweise
Im Deutschen antworten wir auf **Entscheidungsfragen** oft mit einem einfach „Ja" oder „Nein". Im Englischen klingt das komisch, deshalb wird eine Kurzantwort verwendet.

Das muss ich wissen
Im Englischen werden **Entscheidungsfragen** mit *do / does* verwendet, um herauszufinden, ob jemand etwas tut.
Die Entscheidungsfrage beginnt dabei mit dem Hilfsverb *(do)*. Anschließend folgen Subjekt und Vollverb und evtl. auch Ort oder Zeit.
Die Kurzantwort wird mit dem Hilfsverb am Anfang der Frage gebildet, also mit *do*.
Yes, I do. / No, I don't.
Achtung: Bei der 3. Person Singular musst du entsprechend *does* verwenden. Dies gilt auch für die Kurzantwort: *Yes, she does. / No, she doesn't.*

IV. Text Production

Write an email to your friend Emily and tell her about a trip to the restaurant
(You can make up this trip it does not have to be real)
Schreibe eine E-Mail an deine Freundin Emily und erzähle ihr von einem Restaurantbesuch. Du kannst diesen erfinden, er muss nicht wirklich stattgefunden haben. Stell dir einfach vor, wie es war, was du gegessen hast, mit wem du dort warst etc. und berichte Emily davon

Dear Emily,
last week I went to a restaurant with my mum and dad. It was a restaurant with all kinds of pizza. I ate a pizza with mushrooms and tomatoes. There was a birthday party at the table next to us and we all sang 'Happy Birthday' for the lady. She was very nice and ordered cake for everyone – even for us. It was a great evening.
How are you? When do you come to Germany?
I hope to hear from you soon.
Love,
Suzan

3. Schulaufgabe aus dem Englischen

Name: ___________________________

Stoff: Unit 4, Unit 5

I. Reading Comprehension

Read the following text and answer all questions

Lucy, Maya, Sam and Justin are at the supermarket:

Lucy: What do we need?

Maya: Well, we need food for dinner tonight and for breakfast and lunch tomorrow.

Justin: Let's cook hamburger and chips tonight.

Sam: No, I want pasta salad.

Maya: I like mashed potatoes and pasta. And rolls and toast for breakfast.

Lucy: I think we can make a salad. We need lettuce, carrots, tomatoes, mushrooms, cheese and some grapes.

Sam: Grapes in a salad, are you crazy?

Lucy: No, it is great. We can buy toast and cereals for breakfast.

Justin: What about lunch? I want lemonade or orange juice.

Maya: And water. I think some fruit is good. Maybe apples, pears and strawberries.

Sam: But I want pasta salad.

Lucy: No Sam. A regular salad is better.

Justin: What about chips?

Maya: Let's buy chips.

Lucy: Alright, some chips for Justin and Sam and I forgot the cucumber for our salad.

Maya: Yes, cucumber and tomatoes of course. Maybe some sausages that we can cut?

Lucy: Ok, so we eat salad and toast for dinner, cereals and rolls for breakfast and chips and toast for lunch.

Justin, Sam and Maya: Ok.

1. What does Sam want to buy for dinner?

He want to have pasta salad.

2. Which special ingredient (=Zutat) does Lucy want for the salad?

She wants to grapes.

3. Which ingredients do they buy for the salad?

____

4. What do they eat for lunch?

____

5. What does Maya like for breakfast?

____

____/12

II. Vocabulary

1. Write a complete sentence using the vocabulary word

a) answer: ______________________________________

b) weather: ______________________________________

c) market: ______________________________________

d) bottle: ______________________________________

e) feel: ______________________________________

____/10

2. Give the opposite of the following words

a) to be right ↔ ________________

b) expensive ↔ ________________

c) to buy ↔ ________________

d) happy ↔ ________________

e) to leave a message ↔ ________________

____/5

III. Grammar

1. Translate the following sentences into English

a) Was machst du gerade?

____

b) Ich sitze im Café mit Linda und Tommy.

____

c) Sie organisiert gerade die Party.

____

d) Was macht deine Mutter heute?

____

e) Spielst du gerade mit deinem Bruder?

____

____/15

IV. Composition

Write a conversation between a tourist (Sam) and a woman from Paris. Use the information here and write their questions and answers
Schreibe eine Unterhaltung zwischen einem Touristen (Sam) und einer Frau aus Paris. Nutze die Informationen, um ihre Fragen und Antworten zu schreiben

- Ja, ich spreche Englisch.
- Natürlich, wie kann ich dir denn helfen?
- Du musst den Bus 45 zum Flughafen nehmen.
- Du findest ihn auf der anderen Seite der Straße.
- Kein Problem. Einen schönen Tag!

Sam: Excuse me, do you speak English?
Woman: ____
Sam: ____
Woman: ____
Sam: ____
Woman: ____
Sam: ____
Woman: ____
Sam: ____
Woman: ____
Sam: ____

____/20

Total ____/62

Good luck !

Lösung: 3. Schulaufgabe aus dem Englischen

I. Reading Comprehension

Read the following text and answer all questions

Lucy, Maya, Sam and Justin are at the supermarket:

Lucy: What do we need?

Maya: Well, we need food for dinner tonight and for breakfast and lunch tomorrow.

Justin: Let's cook hamburgers and chips tonight.

Sam: No, I want pasta, salad.

Maya: I like mashed potatoes and pasta. And rolls and toast for breakfast.

Lucy: I think we can make a salad. We need lettuce, carrots, tomatoes, peppers, mushrooms, cheese and some grapes.

Sam: Grapes in a salad, are you crazy?

Lucy: No, it is great. We can buy toast and cereals for breakfast.

Justin: What about lunch? I want lemonade or orange juice.

Maya: And water. I think some fruit is good. Maybe apples, pears and strawberries.

Sam: But I want pasta salad.

Lucy: No Sam. A regular salad is better.

Justin: What about chips?

Maya: Let's buy chips.

Lucy: Alright, some chips for Justin and Sam and I forgot the cucumber for our salad.

Maya: Yes, cucumber and tomatoes of course. Maybe some sausages that we can cut?

Lucy: Ok, so we eat salad and toast for dinner, cereals and rolls for breakfast and chips and toast for lunch.

Justin, Sam and Maya: Ok.

1. What does Sam want to buy for dinner?

Sam wants pasta salad.

2. Which special ingredient (=Zutat) does Lucy want for the salad?

She wants grapes in the salad.

3. Which ingredients do they buy for the salad?

They buy sausages, lettuce, cucumber, tomatoes, carrots, mushrooms, cheese and grapes.

4. What do they eat for lunch?

They eat chips and toast for lunch.

5. What does Maya like for breakfast?

Maya likes rolls and toast for breakfast.

II. Vocabulary

1. Write a complete sentence using the vocabulary word

a) answer: *The answer to your question is no.*

b) weather: *In London the weather was nice.*

c) market: *Can you buy apples at the market, please?*

d) bottle: *I forgot my bottle at home.*

e) feel: *I feel very good today.*

2. Give the opposite of the following words

a) to be right ↔ *to be wrong*

b) expensive ↔ *cheap*

c) to buy ↔ *to sell*

d) happy ↔ *sad*

e) to leave a message ↔ *to take a message*

Tipps und Hinweise
Wenn du Vokabeln lernst, bringe sie immer direkt in eine Ordnung.
Du kannst dir Wörter z.B. in folgenden Ordnungen merken:
– **gegensätzliche Bedeutung**: z.B. *big* ↔ *small*
– **mehrere Schreibweisen / Variationen für ein Wort** (gleiche Bedeutung): *grandfather, grandpa*
– **mehrere Bedeutungen** für ein Wort: *the look, to look at, to look good / happy / angry...*
Manchmal musst du gut aufpassen, denn beim Übersetzen können sich leicht Fehler einschleichen!

III. Grammar

1. Translate the following sentences into English

a) Was machst du gerade?

What are you doing (right now)?

b) Ich sitze im Café mit Linda und Tommy.

I am sitting in a café with Linda and Tommy.

c) Sie organisiert gerade die Party.

She is organizing a party (right now).

d) Was macht deine Mutter heute?

What is your mum doing today?

e) Spielst du gerade mit deinem Bruder?

Are you playing with your brother (right now)?

Das muss ich wissen
Die **Verlaufsform der Gegenwart** ***(present progressive)*** bezieht sich auf die Gegenwart.
Sie wird verwendet, um zu sagen, was jemand jetzt gerade tut oder was gerade passiert. Es ist also eine Handlung, die zum Zeitpunkt der Aussage noch nicht abgeschlossen ist.
Gebildet wird das ***present progressive*** mit der entsprechenden Form von *to be: am / are / is +* ***-ing*****-Form des Verbs**
Die **-*ing*-Form** wird gebildet durch **Infinitiv** + *ing*: z.B. *play + ing → playing*
Die **verneinte Form** des ***present progressive*** bildest du aus der Form von *(to) be + not +* **-*ing*-Form**: *I am not playing piano. She is not talking to her mum.*
Bei **Entscheidungsfragen** wird das Subjekt mit der Form von *(to) be* getauscht: *You are dancing. → Are you dancing? She is going to the party. → Is she going to the party?*
Bei **Fragen mit Fragewort** steht dieses an erster Stelle. Ansonsten ist die Reihenfolge der Wörter gleich wie bei Entscheidungsfragen. *Where are you going? What are you doing?*

Tipps und Hinweise
Wie immer gibt es auch beim ***present progressive*** ein paar Ausnahmen, die du dir gut merken solltest:
– Endet ein Verb auf ein stummes ***e*** wie z.B. *organize* fällt dieses in der **-*ing*-Form** weg:
organize → organizing *come → coming*
– Endet ein Verb auf einem kurzen Vokal + Konsonant, wird dieser bei der **-*ing*-Form** verdoppelt: *swim → swimming* *run → running*

IV. Composition

Write a conversation between a tourist (Sam) and a woman from Paris. Use the information here and write their questions and answers
Schreibe eine Unterhaltung zwischen einem Touristen (Sam) und einer Frau aus Paris. Nutze die Informationen, um ihre Fragen und Antworten zu schreiben

- Ja, ich spreche Englisch.
- Natürlich, wie kann ich dir denn helfen?
- Du musst den Bus 45 zum Flughafen nehmen.
- Du findest ihn auf der anderen Seite der Straße.
- Kein Problem. Einen schönen Tag!

Sam: Excuse me, do you speak English?

Woman: Yes, I speak English.

Sam: Can you help me, please?

Woman: Of course, how can I help you?

Sam: How do I get to the airport?

Woman: The number 45 bus goes there.

Sam: Ok, and where can I find the number 45 bus?

Woman: You find it on the other side of the street, over there.

Sam: Thank you so much for your help.

Woman: No problem. Have a great day.

Sam: Thanks.

3. Schulaufgabe aus dem Englischen

Name: ______________________________

Stoff: Unit 4, Unit 5

I. Listening Comprehension

Listen to the text and answer all questions ***(Text aus Lösung 2x vorlesen lassen)***

a) What is the name of the company (=Firma) that the text is about?

The ~~mo~~ name is Active Fit Studio.

b) What sport classes do they offer? Name at least five.

A sailing class, swimming or dancing lessons you can go skating and they even know how to ride horses

c) What happens on Thursday?

There's no special offer on Thursday

d) Why should you buy a ticket for the classes now?

____

____

____/10

II. Vocabulary

1. Explain these words in English, please! ***Erkläre diese Wörter auf Englisch***

a) survey: ______________________________

b) to shout: ______________________________

c) juice: ______________________________

d) garage: ______________________________

e) bargain: ______________________________ ____/10

2. Complete the sentence and write down five places where you can buy things

You can buy things things…. ______________________

You can buy things things…. ______________________

You can buy things things…. ______________________

You can buy things things… ______________________

You can buy things things… ______________________

____/5

III. Grammar

1. Translate these sentences into English using the correct quantifiers *(Mengenwörter)*

a) Ich habe ein paar Spielsachen für deinen kleinen Bruder.

____

b) Kannst du mir etwas Geld geben?

____

c) Hast du ein bisschen Zeit für mich, Annie?

____

d) Das Sweatshirt ist ein paar Pfund wert.

____

e) Hier sind ein paar CDs für dich.

____

____/15

2. Fill in the blanks with *some* – *any* and *no*

"Mandy, do you have __any__ films that we can watch?" – "No, I haven't got __any__ films that we can watch but I have __some__ games that we can play."

"Are there __any__ fruits in the basket?" – "There are __~~some~~ no__ fruits here but I saw __some__ in the kitchen."

"I need __some__ money for new clothes, I don't have __any__ left in my bank account."

"Would you like __some__ cheese for your pasta?" – "Yes, I will take __some__."

____/5

IV. Text Production

What are you wearing today? Write a short text about what you are wearing today. You can give some extra information like colours, where you bought your clothes etc.
Was hast du heute an? Schreibe einen kurzen Text darüber, was du heute an hast. Du kannst ein paar extra Informationen wie Farbe, wo du es gekauft hast, etc. geben

____/15

Total ____/61

Good luck !

Lösung: 3. Schulaufgabe aus dem Englischen

I. Listening Comprehension

Listen to the text and answer all questions *(Text 2x vorlesen lassen)*

Welcome to Active Fit Studio. We have all kinds of sporty activities for you. And we have special price for you. You only pay half the costs. Do you want to join our gymnastics class or do yoga, kung fu or judo? You can also play basketball, football, tennis or other ball games. We offer a sailing class, swimming or dancing lessons. You can go skating with our teachers and they even know how to ride horses. So what is it that you want to do at Active Fit Studio? Let us know and buy your tickets for the classes today! Our special offer ends on Wednesday and classes will sell for the full price starting Thursday.

a) What is the name of the company (=Firma) that the text is about?
The name of the company is Active Fit Studio
b) What sport classes do they offer? Name at least five.
They offer yoga, kung fu, basketball, football, tennis, sailing, swimming, skating, gymnastics, judo and dance classes.
c) What happens on Thursday?
On Thursday classes will cost the full price and the special offer ends.
d) Why should you buy a ticket for the classes now?
Because the classes now only cost half the money.

II. Vocabulary

1. Explain these words in English, please! *Erkläre diese Wörter auf Englisch*
a) survey: *With a survey, you can find out what people think.*
b) to shout: *When I shout, I talk very loud.*
c) juice: *A juice is a drink made of fruits.*
d) garage: *A garage is a room where you can park the car. / Many people park their car in a garage.*
e) bargain: *A bargain is something that didn't cost a lot. / A bargain is something that is very cheap.*

2. Complete the sentence and write down five places where you can buy things
You can buy things… *at a supermarket*
at a flea market
in a shoe shop
in a jewellery shop
in a book shop
in a bakery
in a shop.

Tipps und Hinweise
Hier darfst du wirklich kreativ sein und einfach fünf Orte aufschreiben, an denen du Dinge kaufen kannst. Das können Sachen sein wie Kleidung, Essen, Autos … ganz egal.

III. Grammar

1. Translate these sentences into English using the correct quantifiers *(Mengenwörter)*

a) Ich habe ein paar Spielsachen für deinen kleinen Bruder.

I have some toys for your little brother.

b) Kannst du mir etwas Geld geben?

Can you give me a little money?

c) Hast du ein bisschen Zeit für mich, Annie?

Do you have a little time for me, Annie?

d) Das Sweatshirt ist ein paar Pfund wert.

The sweatshirt is worth a couple of pounds.

e) Hier sind ein paar CDs für dich.

Here are a few CDs for you.

Das muss ich wissen
Die **Mengenwörter** *a few, a couple of* und *a little* nutzt du, um zu sagen, dass "einige", "ein paar" oder "ein bisschen" von etwas vorhanden ist.
Vor zählbaren Personen und Dingen im Plural verwendest du *a few* oder *a couple of*:
I have a few toys. I have a couple of toys.
Vor nicht zählbaren Nomen im Singular verwendest du *a little*.
A little time, a little money...
Nach *a few, a couple* und *a little* kannst du das Nomen in einer Antwort weglassen.
z.B. *Do you need a few toys? – Yes, I need a few.*

2. Fill in the blanks with *some – any* and *no*

"Mandy, do you have *any* films that we can watch?" – "No, I haven't got *any* films that we can watch but I have *some* games that we can play."

"Are there *any* fruits in the basket?" – "There are *no* fruits here but I saw *some* in the kitchen."

"I need *some* money for new clothes, I don't have *any* left in my bank account."

"Would you like *some* cheese for your pasta?" – "Yes, I will take *some*."

Das muss ich wissen
Some und *any* benutzt du immer dann, wenn du keine genaue Mengenangabe machen kannst. Du kannst *some* und *any* bzw. *not... any* oder *no* im Englischen vor **zählbaren Nomen im Plural** wie z.B. *books, DVDs* und vor **nicht zählbaren Nomen** z.B. *clothes, hair, money* verwenden.
Merke dir:
– ***some*** wird benutzt, um zu sagen, dass etwas vorhanden ist.
– ***some*** wird verwendet, wenn du eine höfliche Bitte oder Frage, ein Angebot oder Vorschlag machst und eine positive Antwort erwartest (z.B. *Would you like some cheese with that?*)
– ***any*** benutzt du, wenn du Fragen stellst.
– ***any*** benutzt du, wenn du etwas verneinst.
– Anstelle von ***not... any*** kannst du auch einfach ***no*** verwenden: *There aren't any books here. = There are no books here.*

IV. Text Production

What are you wearing today? Write a short text about what you are wearing today. You can give some extra information like colours, where you bought your clothes etc.
Was hast du heute an? Schreibe einen kurzen Text darüber, was du heute an hast. Du kannst ein paar extra Informationen wie Farbe, wo du es gekauft hast, etc. geben

Today I am wearing my favourite blue jeans. I am also wearing a grey T-shirt and my blue sneakers. My socks are green and yellow and my jacket is dark green. I am wearing a bracelet that my mum gave me for my birthday.

Today I am wearing blue shorts and a black T-shirt. I am wearing sandals and my base cap. I bought it in New York City when I was on vacation. I am wearing a blue jacket and my sunglasses.

4. Schulaufgabe aus dem Englischen

Name: ______________________________

Stoff: Unit 5, Unit 6

I. Listening Comprehension

Listen to the text and answer all questions ***(Text aus Lösung 2x vorlesen lassen)***

Tick off all the correct answers: Attention, sometimes more than one answer is correct

1. English is spoken as a first language in these countries:
□ United States of America
□ Nigeria
□ Australia
□ New Zealand
□ Canada

2. English is an official language.
□ Germany
□ India
□ South Sudan
□ France
□ Pakistan

3. How many people speak English as their first language?
□ 357 million
□ 375 million
□ 357 billion
□ 375 billion
□ none

____/15

II. Vocabulary

1. Write down these ordinal numbers

1st: ____________________________

9th: ____________________________

12th: ____________________________

19th: ____________________________

30th: ____________________________

40th: ____________________________

54th: ____________________________

100th: ____________________________

____/8

2. Complete the table and fill in the German, American English or British English words missing

German	British English	American English
	garden	
		soccer
Zentrum		
		vacation
	colour	
Pommes frites		
Theater		
	mum	

____/8

III. Grammar

Translate these sentences into English or German

a) Ich muss unbedingt meine Oma anrufen.

____

b) Ich darf den Geburtstagskuchen nicht vergessen.

____

c) You needn't buy any milk.

____

d) You mustn't talk to strangers.

____

e) Du musst dir diesen Film unbedingt ansehen.

____

____/15

IV. Text Production

Write a short text about your last birthday. What was it like? Did you celebrate? Who was invited? What did you eat? You can tell anything you would like. Write at least seven sentences

____

____

____

____

____

____

____

____/20

Total ____/66

Good luck !

Lösung: 4. Schulaufgabe aus dem Englischen

I. Listening Comprehension

Listen to the text and answer all questions *(Text 2x vorlesen lassen)*

English is spoken all over the world. Many people in all parts of the world use English to communicate with each other. In Canada, Australia, New Zealand, Ireland, the United States of America and the United Kingdom most people speak English as their first language. Other countries such as South Sudan, India, Pakistan or Nigeria have English as an official language. English is the first language of about 375 million people.
Many people speak English when they are on holiday or at work. Many pupils learn English in school.

Tick off all the correct answers: Attention, sometimes more than one answer is correct
1. English is spoken as a first language in these countries:
x United States of America
□ Nigeria
x Australia
x New Zealand
x Canada

2. English is an official language.
□ Germany
x India
x South Sudan
□ France
x Pakistan

3. How many people speak English as their first language?
□ 357 million
x 375 million
□ 357 billion
□ 375 billion
□ none

II. Vocabulary

1. Write down these ordinal numbers

1st: *first*

9th: *ninth*

12th: *twelfth*

19th: *nineteenth*

30th: *thirtieth*

40th: *forthieth*

54th: *fifty-fourth*

100th: *(one) hundredth*

2. Complete the table and fill in the German, American English or British English words missing

German	British English	American English
Garten	garden	*yard*
Fußball	*football*	soccer
Zentrum	*centre*	*center*
Ferien	*holiday*	vacation
Farbe	colour	*color*
Pommes frites	*chips*	*fries*
Theater	*theatre*	*theater*
Mutter	mum	*mom*

Tipps und Hinweise
Im **British** und **American English** gibt es manchmal verschiedene Worte für dasselbe Ding. Ebenso gibt es Worte, die gleich sind, aber verschieden geschrieben werden.
Auch das Datum ist verschieden: British English z.B. *4th July* und American English *July 4th*.

III. Grammar

Translate these sentences into English or German

a) Ich muss unbedingt meine Oma anrufen.

I must call my grandma.

b) Ich darf den Geburtstagskuchen nicht vergessen.

I mustn't forget the birthday cake.

c) You needn't buy any milk.

Du brauchst keine Milch zu kaufen.

d) You mustn't talk to strangers.

Du darfst nicht mit Fremden sprechen.

e) Du musst dir diesen Film unbedingt ansehen.

You must watch this film.

Das muss ich wissen
Das Modalverb *must* benutzt du, um zu sagen, dass etwas notwendig oder wichtig ist.
Das Modalverb *needn't* wird verwendet, um zu sagen, dass etwas nicht notwendig ist.
Das Modalverb *mustn't* wird verwendet, um zu sagen, dass jemand etwas nicht darf.
Du drückst also ein Verbot aus.
Die **Modalverben** *must, mustn't* und *needn't* sind für alle Personen gleich.
Außer in der Kurzform können im Englischen die Modalverben nicht ohne Vollverb vorkommen.

IV. Text Production

Write a short text about your last birthday. What was it like? Did you celebrate? Who was invited? What did you eat? You can tell anything you would like. Write at least seven sentences

My birthday is on May 26th. For my last birthday I had a birthday party with my friends. It was a lot of fun. We celebrated in the garden with a big picnic. My brother and sisters sang "Happy Birthday". My mum made a birthday cake for me. It was delicious. I enjoyed the good and warm weather. I love my birthday.

4. Schulaufgabe aus dem Englischen

Name: ___________________________

Stoff: Unit 5, Unit 6

I. Dictation

(Text aus Lösung erst 1x komplett vorlesen lassen und dann Satz für Satz diktieren)

____

____

____

____

____

____

____

____

____/15

II. Vocabulary

Translate into English

a) Du darfst nicht zu Schule gehen.

____

b) Du musst nicht zur Schule gehen.

____

c) Ich will, dass du zur Schule gehst.

____

d) Die Übernachtung ist am 14. Oktober.

____

e) Ohne meinen Handschuh kann ich nicht gewinnen.

____

f) Ich mag keine Kirschen aus der Dose. Ich mag nur frische Kirschen.

____

g) Ich stolperte über den Hund und tat mir weh.

____

h) Lass uns bis Mitternacht aufbleiben.

____ ____/16

III. Grammar

Fill in the table with the correct forms of the verbs

Infinitiv	**Simple past form**
(to) do	
	ate
(to) make	
(to) swim	
	thought
(to) meet	
	wrote
	tried
(to) forget	
	visited
(to) hear	
	fed
	said
(to) run	
(to) save	
(to) look	

____/16

IV. Composition

Ludo schreibt seiner Tante Monika einen Brief. Er erzählt ihr, dass er gerade in den Ferien in Berlin ist. Er sagt, dass er im Gästehaus *(guest house)* im Wohnzimmer sitzt. Er fragt seine Tante, wie es ihr geht. Er erzählt, dass er eine tolle Zeit in Berlin mit seiner Familie hat. Er sagt, er war schon in der Stadt und Einkaufen mit seiner Mutter. Er sagt, dass er eine neue Hose und zwei neue T-Shirts gekauft hat. Er sagt, dass seine Mutter ein neues Kleid gekauft hat. Er fragt seine Tante, ob sie auch in den Ferien wegfährt und wann sie sich wieder sehen werden. Er richtet Grüße von seinen Eltern aus.

Write Ludo's letter. Make sure to use the correct time for the verbs. Pay attention to the correct formal aspects of a letter. (Achte auf die formalen Aspekte eines Briefes)

____/20

Total: ____/67

Good luck !

Lösung: 4. Schulaufgabe aus dem Englischen

I. Dictation

(Text erst 1x komplett vorlesen lassen und dann Satz für Satz diktieren)

It is Maya's birthday next week. She writes invitations to her friends. Her birthday is on Monday. Maya's mum bakes cake and buys biscuits. Maya has twelve candles on her birthday cake. The kids play in the garden. Later they go to the zoo and eat pizza. Maya's dad plays games with them.

II. Vocabulary

Translate into English

a) Du darfst nicht zur Schule gehen.

You mustn't go to school.

b) Du musst nicht zur Schule gehen.

You needn't go to school.

c) Ich will, dass du zur Schule gehst.

I want you to go to school.

d) Die Übernachtung ist am 14. Oktober.

The sleepover is on 14th October.

e) Ohne meinen Handschuh kann ich nicht gewinnen.

I can't win without my glove.

f) Ich mag keine Kirschen aus der Dose. Ich mag nur frische Kirschen.

I don't like tinned cherries. I only like fresh cherries.

g) Ich stolperte über den Hund und tat mir weh.

I tripped over the dog and hurt myself.

h) Lass uns bis Mitternacht aufbleiben.

Let's stay up until midnight.

III. Grammar

Fill in the table with the correct forms of the verbs

Infinitiv	**Simple past form**
(to) do	*did*
(to) eat	ate
(to) make	*made*

(to) swim	*swam*
(to) think	thought
(to) meet	*met*
(to) write	wrote
(to) try	tried
(to) forget	*forgot*
(to) visit	visited
(to) hear	*heard*
(to) feed	fed
(to) say	said
(to) run	*ran*
(to) save	*saved*
(to) look	*looked*

Das muss ich wissen
Die **einfache Form der Vergangenheit** ***(simple past)*** wird in der Regel gebildet, indem du den Verben ein ***ed*** an den **Infinitiv** hängst.
z.B. *to play → played*
Diese gebildete Form wird dann für alle Personen verwendet.
Also: ***I / you / he / she / it / we / you / they*** *played in the snow.*
Es gibt aber auch **Sonderformen**:
Bei Verben mit stummem **e** am Ende z.B. *arrive* fällt dieses weg → *arrived*
Bei Verben mit einzelnem betontem Vokal wird der Konsonant verdoppelt z.B. *stop → stopped*
Bei Verben mit *y* nach Konsonant verändert sich dieses zu einem *ied → to try → tried*
Unregelmäßige Verben: Es gibt einige Verben, bei denen die Vergangenheitsform unregelmäßig ist. Diese musst du auswendig lernen: z.B. *to go → went* oder *to come → came*

IV. Composition

Ludo schreibt seiner Tante Monika einen Brief. Er erzählt ihr, dass er gerade in den Ferien in Berlin ist. Er sagt, dass er im Gästehaus *(guest house)* im Wohnzimmer sitzt. Er fragt seine Tante, wie es ihr geht. Er erzählt, dass er eine tolle Zeit in Berlin mit seiner Familie hat. Er sagt, er war schon in der Stadt und Einkaufen mit seiner Mutter. Er sagt, dass er eine neue Hose und zwei neue T-Shirts gekauft hat. Er sagt, dass seine Mutter ein neues Kleid gekauft hat. Er fragt seine Tante, ob sie auch in den Ferien wegfährt und wann sie sich wieder sehen werden. Er richtet Grüße von seinen Eltern aus.
Write Ludo's letter. Make sure to use the correct time for the verbs. Pay attention to the correct formal aspects of a letter. (Achte auf die formalen Aspekte eines Briefes)

3rd June 2017

Dear Monika,

I am on holiday in Berlin. Right now I am sitting in the living room of our guest house. How are you doing? I am having a great time in Berlin with my family. I went to the city and I went shopping with my mum. I bought a new pair of pants and two t-shirts. Mum bought herself a new dress. Are you going on holiday? When are we going to see each other again? Mum and dad say hello.

I hope to hear from you soon.

Love,

Ludo

Monika und Claus Arndt aus Waldtrudering geben im Eigenverlag Lernhilfen für Schüler heraus

Die Durchblick-Garanten

Die Tage sind gezählt bis zu den Sommerferien. Nicht alle Schüler jedoch tun sechs Wochen lang nichts für die Schule. Und es gibt so einige Eltern, die sich jetzt schon fürs neue Schuljahr rüsten. Viele von ihnen landen bei Monika und Claus Arndt aus Waldtrudering. Das Ehepaar gibt Hefte mit Schulproben für Grundschüler und Schulaufgaben für Gymnasiasten und Realschüler heraus. Kinder und Jugendliche können sich mit ihren Durchblicker-Aufgaben auf Prüfungen vorbereiten.

Monika und Claus Arndt im Keller ihres Waldtruderinger Hauses. Dort drucken sie ihre Durchblicker-Schulaufgaben. Jahrelang haben sie zudem Nachhilfeunterricht gegeben, mittlerweile konzentrieren sie sich auf ihr Verlagsgeschäft. Ihre Schulaufgaben sind im Buchhandel zu finden und helfen Schülern bei der Lösung von Schulaufgaben. ***Fotos: Panthermedia/ve/kn***

Im Keller der Familie Arndt im Birkhahnweg in Waldtrudering läuft der Drucker. In den Regalen stapeln sich ordentlich die Ausdrucke. Ihre Bestellungen erreichen Monika und Claus Arndt meist spät abends. Nach Ladenschluss schicken Buchhändler noch ihre Bestellliste ab, so auch an den Durchblicker Verlag in Waldtrudering. Viele Jahre lang haben die Arndts im Keller Schülern Nachhilfeunterricht gegeben. Vor fünf Jahren haben sie einen Verlag gegründet und verkaufen seitdem Bücher mit typischen Schulaufgaben für bayerische Schüler. Derzeit, kurz vor den Sommerferien und vor allem dann im September, sei die Nachfrage besonders groß. „Wir haben ein saisonales Geschäft", sagt Claus Arndt schmunzelnd. Bevor es in die Ferien geht oder zum Start ins neue Schuljahr, bestellen Schüler und ihre Eltern die Durchblicker-Schulaufgaben.

Der Mathematiker sattelte aufs Lehramt um

Die Arndts haben sozusagen eine Marktlücke entdeckt: Verlage bieten zwar immer mehr Lernhilfen für Schüler an. Doch die Arndts haben ihre Ausgaben auf die jeweiligen Schultypen und auf die neuen Lehrpläne in Bayern zugeschnitten. So läuft und läuft ihr Drucker. „Volltreffer!", hat ihnen ein Schüler geschrieben, „drei Aufgaben in meiner Schulaufgabe waren genau wie die aus Ihrem Buch!" Und eine Buchhändlerin lässt sie wissen: „Ich empfehle die Reihe immer weiter. Sie haben in mir einen Fan gefunden."

Wie aber kommt es, dass die beiden Waldtruderinger so einen guten Riecher haben, wie Lehrer ihre Schulaufgaben gestalten und was sie wollen? Claus Arndt war als Diplom-Mathematiker in der EDV-Branche beschäftigt. Bis 2004. Da hieß es: „Wer gehen wolle, könne gehen." Der Waldtruderinger Vater zweier Söhne ließ sich das nicht zwei Mal sagen. Händeringend wurde damals nach Lehrern gesucht. So sattelte der Mathematiker kurzerhand um und unterrichtete fortan an der Realschule in Dachau und am Neuperlacher Heinrich-Heine-Gymnasium Mathe.

Damit nicht genug. Zuhause im Keller eröffnete er mit seiner Frau Monika ein Lernstudio für Schüler. Claus Arndt gab Nachhilfe in Mathematik. Seine Frau in Englisch, Deutsch und Französisch. „Für Physik und Latein beschäftigten wir noch weitere Nachhilfelehrer", erzählt Claus Arndt. Die Waldtruderinger Familien nahmen das Angebot gerne an: Bei den Arndts gab es Nachhilfe für den Achtklässler, der darum kämpfte, wegen Mathe bloß nicht durchzufallen. Ein anderer Bub, ein Grundschüler, konnte partout nicht stillsitzen. „Ich ließ ihn hier unten auf einem kleinen Trampolin auf- und abspringen und fragte ihn dabei das Einmaleins ab", erzählt Claus Arndt. Ebenso ackerten gleich mehrere Schüler in einem Crashkurs, um in ihrer Abschlussprüfung eine bessere Note zu bekommen.

Nachhilfeunterricht von 13 bis 20 Uhr

Vier Jahre lang büffelten die Nachhilfelehrer mit ihren Schützlingen Stunde für Stunde im Keller. „Unseren Höhepunkt hatten wir im Jahr 2008, da saßen wir von 13 bis 20 Uhr in unserem Lernstudio, die Nachfrage in Waldtrudering und Umgebung war einfach so groß", erinnert sich Claus Arndt. Was ist das Arndtsche Erfolgsrezept" Die Arndts lösen mit ihren Schülern Schulaufgaben, erarbeiten Musterlösungen und korrigieren die Antworten gemeinsam. „Diese Klassenarbeiten denken wir uns selbst aus", sagt Claus Arndt. Im Laufe der Jahre haben sie ein Gespür dafür entwickelt, welche Aufgabentypen drankommen können — „wie die Lehrer ticken".

Schulaufgaben zu entwickeln, das machte Claus Arndt bald nicht nur für seine Nachhilfeschüler im Münchner Osten. Für die Verlage Klett und Cornelsen modifizierte er Schulaufgaben. „Doch die Lehrpläne variieren von Bundesland zu Bundesland", erzählt der Klausuren-Profi. Und so schlug man ihm vor, für Bayern einfach selbst Schulaufgaben herauszugeben. Im Eigenverlag.

Claus Arndt hatte ja mit seiner Frau Monika kompetente Hilfe an seiner Seite. Denn vor allem sie war es, die in ganz Bayern Buchhändler abklapperte, um Werbung für die Durchblicker-Schulaufgaben zu machen. Mehr noch: Monika Arndt hatte als Autorin bereits Ernährungsbücher für Kinder veröffentlicht, hatte unter anderem beim Stark-Verlag über Produktion sowie Inhalt von Lernhilfen viele Erfahrungen gesammelt und als Lektorin gearbeitet. Sie knöpfte sich nun die Fächer Deutsch, Französisch und Englisch vor und arbeitete ebenso Schulaufgaben aus. Zudem sei es für sie als Schulaufgaben-Entwickler mit Einführung des G8 leichter geworden: „Alles ist systematischer und strukturierter, ich kann eher abschätzen, was in einer Klassenarbeit drankommt", sagt Claus Arndt.

Neu im Angebot sind Proben für Grundschüler

Mittlerweile haben sie eine breite Palette mit 57 verschiedenen Ausgaben im Angebot: Ob für Gymnasiasten Mathe-Schulaufgaben von der fünften bis hoch zur zwölften Klasse oder für Realschüler Englisch-Schulaufgaben. „Und neu und sehr beliebt sind unsere Schulproben in Mathe, Deutsch und HSU für Dritt- und Viertklässler", sagt Monika Arndt. „Die sind immer mehr unsere Renner!" Als Verlag profitieren sie von dem wachsendem Druck, der schon auf Grundschüler ausgeübt werde. „Eltern wollen unbedingt, dass ihr Kind einen Notendurchschnitt von 2,33 beim Übertrittszeugnis in der vierten Klasse hat, damit es aufs Gymnasium gehen kann", sagt Claus Arndt. „Das ist oft zu viel des Guten." Er weiß, wovon er spricht. Er hat in all den Jahren in seinem Lernstudio viele Kinder kennengelernt. „Oft haben wir gemerkt, welch großen Druck Eltern auf ihr Kind ausüben können." Natürlich müsse sich jedes Kind auf Tests in der Schule vorbereiten. Doch als Eltern zweier Söhne, 1993 und 1996 geboren, wissen sie eben auch, dass ein Kind nicht zu viel lernen dürfe. „Wer für eine Schulaufgabe mit zwei unserer Aufgaben übt, dem reicht das meist", behauptet Monika Arndt.

Den beiden Schulaufgaben- und Nachhilfe-Profis geht es vor allem darum, Schüler besser auf das vorzubereiten, was sie bei einer Probe erwartet. „Angst und Nervosität legen sich schnell, wenn Schüler ähnliche Aufgaben kennen und bereits bearbeitet haben", sagt Claus Arndt.

Verena Rudolf

Telefon (089) 53 06-420
lokales@merkur.de
Telefax: (089) 53 06-86 56

Mehr Durchblick für Schüler

Claus und Monika Arndt produzieren Lernhefte im heimischen Keller in Waldtrudering

VON LAURA MÜLLER

Vielen Kindern graut es vor der Schule. Häufig sind sie unmotiviert und wissen nicht, wie sie sich auf Tests und Schularbeiten vorbereiten sollen. Für diese Problematik gibt es eine Menge Nachhilfelehrer und Bücher, die helfen sollen. Einer der Verlage, die solche Bücher, oder vielmehr Hefte, produzieren, ist der Durchblicker Verlag – ein kleiner Buchverlag, der nur aus dem Ehepaar Claus und Monika Arndt besteht. Er hat sich auf Schulaufgaben und ihre Lösungen spezialisiert. Die Arndts produzieren die Hefte im heimischen Keller in Waldtrudering.

Auf den jungen Schülern lastet eine Menge Druck, sagen die Arndts

Die Nachfrage ist groß: Im Keller von Monika und Claus Arndt stapeln sich die Lernhefte des heimischen Verlags. Alles ist handproduziert, das ist das Markenzeichen des Verlags.
FOTOS: ASTRID SCHMIDHUBER

Claus Arndt, ein ehemaliger Software-Ingenieur, hat den Verlag vor fünf Jahren gegründet. Angefangen hat alles damit, dass Claus Arndt anfing, Nachhilfe zu geben. „Als die Kinder kamen, wollte ich nicht ständig unterwegs sein", erzählte er. „Also habe ich meinen Job gekündigt und Nachhilfe gegeben." Die Schüler kamen gerne zu Claus Arndt, so wurde die Nachfrage irgendwann zu groß. Die Arndts gaben das Lernbüro auf und fingen an, Bücher mit Schulaufgaben und ihren Lösungen zu drucken. Zunächst verkauften sie nur wenige Hefte, doch im vergangenen Jahr waren es schon 20 000. Insgesamt haben sie 58 Bücher verfasst und herausgebracht. Die Arndts sehen sich mittlerweile als „ernst zu nehmende Konkurrenz" für den renommierten Stark-Verlag. Dessen rote Übungsbücher stehen bei vielen Schülern im Regal.

Claus Arndt sammelt seit der Umstellung auf das G8 Schulaufgaben von verschiedenen Schulen. Weil er selbst mal als Lehrer arbeitete, weiß er, was andere Lehrer erwarten. Claus und Monika Arndt orientieren sich bei ihren Aufgaben immer an dem neusten Stand der Lehrpläne.

Die Hefte des Durchblicker-Verlags: Insgesamt 58 Lerntrainer haben die Arndts schon herausgebracht.

Als die Arndts ihren Verlag gründeten, klapperten sie alle möglichen Büchereien ab, um ihre Bücher präsentieren zu können. Monika Arndt hat schon vorher als Lektorin und Autorin gearbeitet. Sie kennt sich in der Branche aus und weiß, wie man hier etwas erreicht. Heute liegen die Bücher des Durchblicker-Verlags etwa in Hugendubel- und Thalia-Filialen aus. „Wir freuen uns, dass unsere Bücher so gut ankommen", sagt Claus Arndt. Am besten verkaufen sich laut den Arndts die Lerntrainer für die Grundschule sowie für die 5. und 6. Klasse Gymnasium. Das verwundert. Claus Arndt erklärt: „Auf den jungen Schülern lastet schon eine Menge Druck."

Am besten verkaufen sich die Lerntrainer für Grundschule und 5. und 6. Klasse

Als die Arndts die Bücher in immer größerer Stückzahl verkauften, stellte sich die Frage, wie sie die Lerntrainer weiter produzieren wollen. Sie entschieden sich, die Bücher selbst zu drucken. „Alles ist handproduziert, das ist unser Markenzeichen", sagt Monika Arndt.

Sie legen Wert darauf, dass ihre Aufgaben schulnah sind und so auch wirklich abgefragt werden könnten. „Außerdem ist es wichtig für uns, die Schüler für das Lernen zu motivieren. Häufig schreiben Kinder schlechte Noten, weil sie zu wenig Selbstvertrauen haben", sagt Claus Arndt. „Wenn die Kinder mit unseren Schultrainern lernen, erkennen sie Aufgaben aus dem Unterricht wieder, das gibt ihnen ein Erfolgserlebnis und motiviert sie." Natürlich könnten die Bücher keine schon vorher entstandenen Wissenslücken schließen, „aber sie helfen, zu vertiefen und zu wiederholen."

AKTUELLES IN KÜRZE

38-Jähriger stirbt nach Drogenkonsum

Ein 38-jähriger Münchner ist am vergangenen Freitag an den Folgen von Kokain- und Alkoholkonsum gestorben. Nach Angaben der Polizei wurde der arbeitslose Münchner am Donnerstag, 17. November, in eine Klinik eingeliefert. Dort musste er reanimiert werden. In seinem Urin wurde ein hoher Kokaingehalt festgestellt. Zudem hatte er eine Alkoholvergiftung. Die Obduktion ergab, dass der 38-Jährige an einer Überdosis Rauschgift gestorben war. Die Polizei schließt Fremdverschulden aus. pm

Rechte und Pflichten von Mietern

Viele Auseinandersetzungen zwischen Vermietern und Mietern resultieren daraus, dass die Parteien ihre Rechte und Pflichten nicht kennen oder diese falsch einschätzen. Die Rechtsanwältin Gisela Weber vom Mieterverein München erläutert bei einem Infoabend im Bauzentrum München, Willy-Brandt-Allee 10, am Dienstag, 13. Dezember, ab 18 Uhr, welche Klauseln Mieter vor der Unterzeichnung eines Formularmietvertrages besonders unter die Lupe nehmen sollten. Sie spricht außerdem die Probleme des Alltags an, die im täglichen Umgang zwischen den Mietvertragsparteien und den Nachbarn auftreten können. Der Eintritt ist frei. do

Schulaufgaben bayerischer Schulen

Mathematik, Physik, Chemie, Englisch, Französisch, Latein, Deutsch

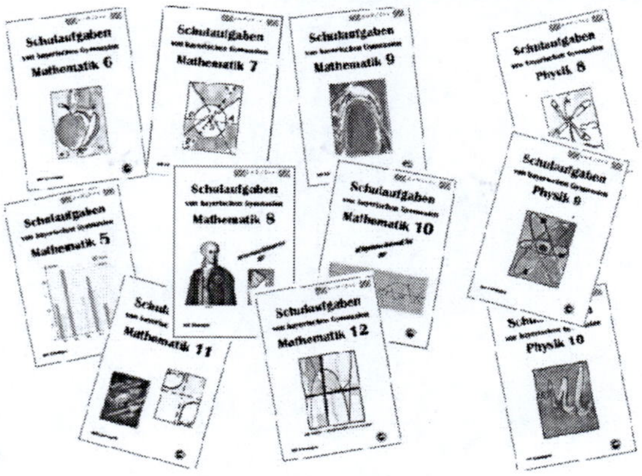

Du willst wissen:

- was in der Schulaufgabe drankommen könnte
- ob du dein Wissen anwenden kannst
- ob du alles in der vorgegebenen Zeit schaffst

- Typische **Schulaufgaben** bayerischer Gymnasien: Darauf muss ich mich einstellen
- Ausführliche **Lösungen**: So sollte meine Antwort aussehen
- Tipps als Hilfestellungen: So kann ich mir die Arbeit erleichtern

☺ **Gymnasium**
Mathematik, Englisch, Deutsch, Franz., Latein, Physik, Chemie

☺ **Realschule**
Mathematik, Englisch, Deutsch

☺ **Grundschule**
HSU, Mathematik, Deutsch

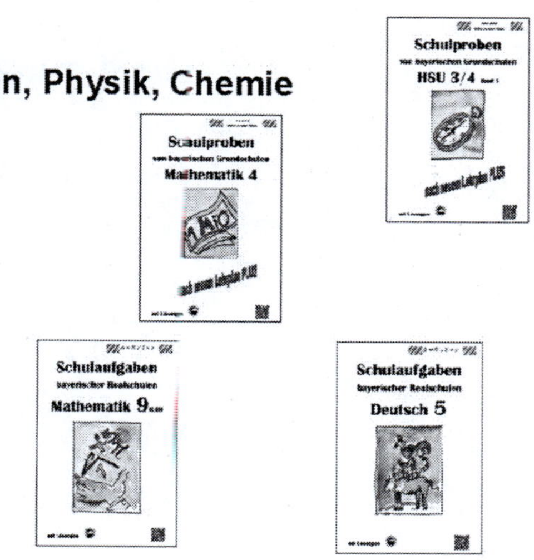

☺ **Zu bestellen siehe unten und im Buchhandel**

☺ **Je Band 14,95 €**

info@durchblicker.org
Tel: 089 - **43 73 73 14**
Fax: 089 – 43 90 60 51

Wir sind engagierte Lehrer mit jahrelanger Nachhilfeerfahrung und machen einen lockeren, aber kompetenten fächerübergreifenden Unterricht. Unsere Spezialität ist die Vorbereitung auf Schulaufgaben.

www.durchblicker.org

S. 17 II
S. 18 ① Textproduktion
S. 23
S. 25
S. 26

„Ein Schüler hat erzählt, dass eine Aufgabe identisch mit Ihrem Heft war. Da haben Sie eine Marktlücke entdeckt. Die Durchblicker sind sehr gefragt. Wir werden geplündert.“
Ein Buchhändler

Mein Sohn Leander hat sich schon letztes Jahr ausschließlich mit Ihren Heften auf seine Schulaufgaben in Mathe und Englisch vorbereitet, was uns zu einem insgesamt recht entspannten ersten Schuljahr im Gymnasium verholfen hat. Wir erleben Ihre Hefte als echte Unterstützung!

Top! Die Schulaufgaben von bayerischen Gymnasien sind wirklich ihr Geld wert. Das gibt den Kindern Sicherheit. Klasse!

„Die Durchblicker Schulaufgaben sind inzwischen unsere Topseller!“
Eine Buchhändlerin

Herzlichen Dank für die prompte Zusendung von Mathematik 11. Martin hat es gut genutzt und 14 Punkte geerntet! Vielen, vielen Dank!

VOLLTREFFER !!!
Drei Aufgaben in meiner Schulaufgabe waren genau wie die aus Ihrem Buch. Ganz toll! Danke!

Großes Lob an Ihr Engagement! Die Hinweise in den ausführlichen Lösungen sind die absoluten Insidertipps!

Wir verwenden die Schulaufgaben für bayerische Gymnasien schon seit einigen Jahren. Die Trainer sind wirklich super. Das ist der Standard, der definitiv in der Schule drankommt.

Wir haben übrigens schon Mathe und Englisch für die 5. Klasse Gymnasium zu Hause und sind total begeistert. Meine Tochter hat schon drei Einser geschrieben.

Die Tipps zu den Matheaufgaben haben meinem Sohn so viel Selbstbewusstsein gegeben, dass er in seiner Schulaufgabe die Note 1 geschrieben hat.

„Ich empfehle die Reihe immer weiter. Sie haben in mir einen Fan gefunden.“
Eine Buchhändlerin

Ihre Bücher sind sensationell, wie ein treuer Wegbegleiter!

Ein dickes Lob! Meine Tochter ist absolut begeistert. Sie hat bei Physik und Chemie das Gefühl: „Das habe ich jetzt verstanden.“

Wir haben alle Ihre Bücher. Die sind spitze!

DURCHBLICKER Lernstudio Arndt

Englisch 5

ISBN: 978-3-00-034520-3

9 783000 345203

€ 14,95 (D) € 15,40 (A)